I0086960

Mademoiselle Renoir
à Paris

Mademoiselle Renoir à Paris

une petite histoire de 1968

Patricia Taylor Wells

GusGus Press • Bedazzled Ink Publishing
Fairfield, California

© 2018 Patricia Taylor Wells

All rights reserved. No part of this publication may be reproduced or
transmitted in any means,
electronic or mechanical, without permission in
writing from the publisher.

978-1-945805-01-1 paperback

Illustrations
by
Charles Hayes

Cover Design
by
Patricia Taylor Wells
&

GusGus Press
a division of
Bedazzled Ink Publishing Company
Fairfield, California
http://www.bedazzledink.com

"First of all, we think the world must be changed. We want the most liberating change of the society and life in which we find ourselves confined. We know that such a change is possible through appropriate actions."

—Guy Debord, 1957, Founding
Member of Situationist International

Mademoiselle Renoir

THE WHOLE WORLD was on fire in 1968. It was not a slow, smoldering camp fire or even a quickly contained brush fire. Nor was it a wildfire sparked by lightning or any other act of God for which no one could be held accountable. It was none of these. Instead, it was a raging fire that enveloped the entire globe, engulfing it in the murky haze of dissent. It began in late January when the North Vietnamese and Viet Cong joined forces in launching coordinated surprise attacks on multiple cities and villages in South Vietnam. News of the Tet Offensive, as it was called because the attacks began on the first day of the Vietnamese lunar New Year known as *Tet*, flabbergasted the American public. The North Vietnamese were not being defeated as they had been led to believe. More troops would be needed, more money spent to continue an undeclared war with questionable strategic importance to the United States. It was a conflict that very few wanted or understood.

The searing image of a handcuffed Viet Cong prisoner being executed by the Saigon Chief of Police was more than they could stomach. And a few weeks later, the My Lai Massacre stunned them even more. US Army soldiers, certain the Viet Cong who had participated in the Tet Offensive were hiding out in the South Vietnamese village of My Lai, attacked and murdered nearly five hundred unarmed men, women, and children thought to be active VC sympathizers. Despite the fact that only a few weapons were found and little if any resistance from villagers was met, the US Army's search-and-destroy mission culminated in the most brutal act against innocent civilians in the Vietnam War.

Violent protests against the Vietnam War erupted throughout the United States and elsewhere in response to these atrocities. But the flames of discontent were not limited to the Vietnam War. Burning and looting occurred in nearly every major city in the US following the assassination of the revered minister and leader of the civil rights movement, Martin Luther King, Jr. Soon after, Robert F. Kennedy, the brother of President John F. Kennedy who was slain on the streets of Dallas five years earlier, was mortally wounded while campaigning for the Democratic nomination for president. The Soviet Union invaded Czechoslovakia in an attempt to quell its feeble crawl toward a more democratic way of life brought on by the Prague Spring, a short-lived movement opposed to the iron-fisted rule of communism. And in France, students and workers joined forces against the government, setting off violent protests and massive strikes that brought the country to a standstill and nearly collapsed it altogether.

I was a freshman in college at the time and knew little of what was going on in the world. There were only two things that mattered to me: my newfound independence and falling in love for the first time. Getting an education was not a priority for me, so consequently, I was not a good student. The only class that held my attention was Intermediate French. I loved the sound of this romantic language and though I can't remember the first time I heard it spoken, I could remember pretending I could speak it when I was as young as ten or eleven. Of course, back then I didn't actually know any words other than *oui, non,* or *oh là là* (pronounced and spelled *ooh la la* by most Americans).

Early in my first semester of college, my French professor, a plump Canadian woman in her early fifties, began to favor me over the other students, even though my language skills weren't as proficient as some of my classmates.

"*Est-ce à ou de, Mademoiselle Renoir?*" Madame Girard articulated each syllable as she pointed to the verbs she had written on the board. No one responded.

"Mademoiselle Renoir?" she asked again as she moved closer to my desk.

I looked around, thinking she had mixed me up with another student. She startled me by thumping the rolled-up paper she held in her hand on my desk.

"I'm speaking to you, Mademoiselle Renoir," Madame Girard confirmed.

"But that's not my name," I said.

"Ah, but to me you are like a Renoir painting; so very fair. The artist himself would agree. I will call you Mademoiselle Renoir from now on. Now tell me which preposition should I use with each of the verbs I wrote on the board, à or *de*?"

I could feel my cheeks burning, and I wanted to crawl under my desk. A couple of the girls in the back of the room were giggling and the boy behind me whispered, "*la chouchou du professeur*" loud enough for those nearby to hear. This was not junior high. I was in college, and I couldn't believe my French professor had chosen me as her pet. I would never live it down. It didn't take me long to determine that my only defense was to do whatever it took to change her opinion of me. I would argue with her, laugh at my classmates when they made mistakes, and wear dresses or skirts that were too short for her standards. But even that backfired.

"Your dress is too short, Mademoiselle Renoir," she would scold. "But on you it looks good."

I finally gave up and learned to live with the nick name. There were advantages to being Madame Girard's favorite student. She was more forgiving when I clearly hadn't studied a lesson, and she rarely asked me anything she knew I couldn't answer.

After a while my classmates were calling me Mademoiselle Renoir, too. Even today, there are a few who still refer to me by that name.

Sometime in mid-spring, Madame Girard approached me with the idea of joining the group of young women she was assembling to study French in Paris that summer at the Sorbonne. This was something she had done for several years. Once classes in Paris were over, the group would travel to different places in Europe before returning home.

"I will serve as the tour guide as well as chaperone, *bien sûr*," she advised me. "You must come with us. Paris awaits you."

"I would love to go, but I don't think my parents would give me permission, let alone cough up the money for a trip overseas."

"You won't know until you try. Write them a letter. Tell them how affordable it is and that you won't be wandering around on your own. It would be a wonderful opportunity for you. Paris is the most beautiful city in the world. You must go there, Mademoiselle Renoir."

The idea of going to Paris took hold of me. I thought of nothing else. I did as Madame Girard suggested and wrote my parents a letter listing ten reasons why I should go to Paris. It was a long shot, but to my surprise, my parents gave me permission. In all probability, their consent was an attempt to appease the strained relationship that had developed between us after my younger brother passed away three years earlier. Even though my going away to college last fall had eased the tension between us somewhat, I was certain my parents would prefer not having me home for the summer. My going to Paris was good for them, too.

There was only one drawback to all my excitement about the trip. I was madly in love with Ted, and I dreaded having to tell him my big news. Our relationship was going well. We spent all of our free time together, hanging out at the local diner where we took advantage of the free refills of coffee. We talked for hours, holding hands and gazing into each other's eyes as if nothing else in the world existed. But there was a dark side to our relationship, too. Ted's brother had died in an automobile accident in the fall, shortly after we met. I sometimes wondered if the reason we were drawn to each other was because we shared a similar life tragedy.

Ted and I had planned on signing up for the summer session. My only reason for skipping vacation was to be with him. Now, all of that had changed. I worried if he would forget all about me if we were not together for several months.

"I need to tell you something," I said after we sat in our favorite booth of the diner one evening.

"What's wrong?" Ted asked.

"Nothing's wrong. It's all good. Only, I don't know how you'll feel about it."

"Just tell me," Ted said. He placed his hand on top of mine.

"I'm going to school in Paris for the summer."

"Paris? Do you mean Paris, Texas or Paris, France?"

"France. Madame Girard is taking a group over to study at the Sorbonne. It's a great opportunity for me."

"Well, that's news. I can't say it makes me happy. When do you leave?"

"The end of June."

"Who all is going?"

"I don't know any of the students who are going. Except Glenda Cole. She's the daughter of Dean Cole. I don't think she's a student though. I heard she was married and had a young child."

"Will there be any guys on the trip?"

"No, only girls. Madame Girard will chaperone us."

"Whatever that means. You need to be careful over there."

"Are you worried about me?"

"I am. There's a white slave market in Europe. Young women are kidnapped and sold into prostitution. Most of the girls don't even realize what's happening to them until it's too late."

"Oh, I don't think anything like that will happen. Not to me, anyway. I'm always careful."

"No you're not. If it weren't for me, you'd be run over every time you crossed the street."

"I don't have to worry about anything when I'm with you."

"That's why I want you to be extra careful. I would go crazy if something happened to you." A warm feeling rushed through me as Ted squeezed my hand. It was good to feel this loved.

"I'll write you every day," I vowed. "That way you'll know I'm safe and sound on the other side of the world."

My plans to study abroad came close to being cancelled due to the political unrest that was occurring throughout France. In May 1968, there were numerous student protests that resulted in the Sorbonne and other universities being shut down. Workers joined the students and the strikes that followed came close to collapsing the government. President Charles de Gaulle tried to stop the protests, but that only enraged the protesters. Things had quickly gotten out of hand and become violent.

The trouble in Paris had actually begun several months before the May riots. Students at the University Of Nanterre on the outskirts of Paris were dissatisfied with overcrowding and the fact there were no coeducational dormitories. Their demands were virtually ignored by the French government. This led to demonstrations that resulted in student arrests, closing of schools, and escalating conflict between the students and civil authorities. The biggest mistake the French government made was to stoke the fires of discontent by confronting the protesters in an attempt to crush them completely rather than allowing them to have their say. The government made little or no effort to meet their demands, which were vaguely expressed by the students in three simple words:

Egalité! Liberté! Sexualité!

Both Ted and my parents continuously voiced their concerns about my safety, but I largely ignored them. I wanted to go to Paris whether there was rioting or not. It would be so disappointing if the trip was cancelled and all of Madame Girard's plans were unraveled. I had not anticipated anything like this. I didn't like having to wait and see what was going to happen.

"Are the riots really that bad?" I asked Madame Girard.

She was cautious with her words. "There is concern, but this should all be over soon. Everyone will tire of this and things will get back to normal. Don't worry. Nothing will keep us from going to Paris."

I hated having to say goodbye to Ted at the end of the semester. I was secretly glad to hear he had decided not to take any courses that summer. His father, a rice farmer, needed him at home. There wouldn't be any girls on the farm to steal his heart away from me. I could go to France without any worries. I already knew he was the man I wanted to marry, so there wasn't any possibility of my meeting someone in France or any part of the world who could take his place.

I had almost a month to prepare for my trip in accordance with Madame Girard's long list of what we would need and what was forbidden for us to bring with us.

"Do not bring shorts or slacks, only dresses," she had insisted. "I want to show the people of Paris what *real* Americans look and act like. Make certain you have your passport in order, and I will need a copy of your medical insurance. You need to be revaccinated for smallpox, too and don't forget to bring your certificate with you."

I received a letter from Madame Girard the middle of June stating there was some anxiety on the part of the university's administration about allowing us to go to Paris because of the political unrest. Word from Paris, however, had confirmed that all was quiet now that the police had retaken the Sorbonne. Although it was no longer occupied by students and other leftists, it was closed for the time being to prevent another takeover. Summer school would still be held, but in a different location. Approval from our university's president would hinge upon the outcome of the elections in France scheduled for June 23.

I worried that my dream of going to Paris could fall apart altogether. It didn't seem fair that I was given an opportunity that may not be realized because a few people in France were unhappy with their situation.

Prior to the election, President de Gaulle had ordered the workers in Paris to return to their jobs, threatening to impose a state of emergency if they did not cooperate. It was a surprise even to President de Gaulle that his party not only won the election, but by a wide margin. After the outcome was announced, a rally was held to demonstrate strong support for the French president. The street demonstrations organized by the national student union came to a standstill and things in general settled down.

Now that the elections were over and the revolution had been averted, our trip could move forward as planned. Three days before departure, I received another letter from Madame Girard letting me know that final approval for the trip had been granted. She also stated that one of the other faculty members had been in Paris since June 4. He had reported that there had been no demonstrations or problems since his arrival. We were advised, however, that should any trouble start up again, we were not to get involved, and we were not to take any pictures of any riots. If we were arrested, we would be on our own. Her letter did little to comfort my parents, but I was thrilled. I was going to Paris.

Climate Change

IF I HAD fully understood or known what was going on in Paris in May 1968, I would have probably opted out of going altogether. Not only did I not have the immediate access to world events we have today via Internet and cell phone, but there was no television in my dorm room at college, and I rarely watched the TV available in the common room. I never read the newspaper and the radio stations I listened to broadcast only a limited amount of news if any at all. As a result, I wasn't fully aware of all the unrest in my own country, let alone what was happening in France.

It seems too simple to think what began as a protest about overcrowding and the lack of coeducational dormitories on a campus outside of Paris would fling open the door of discontent to such a degree across the entirety of France that it nearly shut the country down altogether. History teaches us, though, that change often stems from a single, unassuming event or idea which resonates with the masses and morphs into an unpredictable outcome. Rosa Parks, a young black activist, refusing to give up her bus seat to a white passenger in 1955 comes to mind. Her refusal to obey Alabama's segregation laws led to her arrest for civil disobedience. Who could have known that one day she would be remembered as the first lady of civil rights? Or that chests of tea being thrown overboard in the Boston Harbor in 1773—an act of defiance against the British tax on tea—would be the catalyst for the American Revolution.

The events that spurred the biggest disruption in French Society since the storming of the Bastille in 1789 then should come as no surprise. On March 22, 1968 eight students broke into the Dean's office at Nanterre University, a small, overcrowded campus on the outskirts of Paris. It was built in the 1960s as an extension of the Sorbonne to accommodate a student population that had tripled over a ten year period. The occupation was in protest of the arrest of several students during an anti-Vietnam War rally that had taken place in Paris. The activists managed to occupy the Dean's office for six days. After the police showed up and surrounded the campus, the students published their demands and vacated the building. From that point on, the protesters were known as the *March 22 Movement*. Later on, the leaders of the occupation were ordered to appear before the college's disciplinary board on May 6. Among them was Daniel Cohn-Bendit, a twenty-two-year-old sociology student who, prior to March 22, was a member of a small group of about twenty-five activists who called themselves *les enragés* (angry people)—a name that dates back to the French Revolution. By the end of March, the group had grown to about a thousand members and by May, *les enragés* boasted over ten million participants.

There are several factors that contributed to the uprising that occurred in France. For one, the French university operated as a totally autocratic system. Not only was there no discussion between teachers and students, but the teachers themselves had no say in decisions regarding curriculum and methodology. An overcrowded campus full of students unhappy with their unattractive, uncomfortable facilities added fuel to the fire and provided a steady stream of ready and willing protesters. Most importantly, the generation gap between France's seventy-seven-year-old leader, Charles de Gaulle, and a youth population that refused to be ignored or victimized had a significant impact on what happened in 1968. No one saw what was coming. No one would have guessed that millions of workers disgruntled over low wages and working conditions would join forces with students whose issues centered on coeducational dormitories and overcrowded campuses. About the only thing the two groups had in common was their strong dislike for President de Gaulle and their desire to have him overthrown, even if they had to assassinate him to achieve their objective. *La Monde* journalist Pierre Viansson-Ponté proclaimed that "France is bored" in an editorial he wrote in March of 1968. But soon, that would all change.

May Madness

ON MAY 2, SUBURBAN Nanterre University was shut down following the eviction of several anti-Vietnam demonstrators in an attempt to curtail student unrest. But the closing of Nanterre had the opposite effect. The disgruntled students left the suburbs, taking their grievances with them to the city. At the same time, the news media from around the world was gathering in Paris to cover the Vietnam peace talks that were scheduled in May. Soon, the whole world would know the discontent the students, and later on the workers of France, held for their president and his lack of interest for their concerns.

The next day a small number of students from Nanterre gathered at the Sorbonne to meet with campus activists regarding the disciplinary board meeting that would take place on May 6 to determine the fate of Danny Cohn-Bendit and other leaders for their role in the March 22 Movement. As the crowds grew, anxious college authorities called the police. The police surrounded the University and arrested six hundred students. As news spread, more and more students from all over the city showed up to support the demonstrators. The situation became so out of control that Sorbonne administrators closed down the university for the first time in its seven hundred years of existence.

Fights broke out between the students and riot police. The students overturned and set fire to cars and buses to serve as barricades to protect themselves against the brutal attacks being levied by the police force. Anger among the protesters rose even higher, as did the number of angry students who showed up to lend their support. But things were just warming up.

A few days later on May 6, Cohn-Bendit and the other seven students who had been expelled from Nanterre made their way toward the Sorbonne where they were to appear before the Disciplinary Committee. They sang the communist anthem "L'Internationale" as they passed rows of police who stood by dressed in riot gear in anticipation of trouble. The original French lyrics for the anthem were written by the revolutionary socialist and poet Eugène Pottier in 1871. The title of the hymn comes from The International Workingmen's Association, commonly referred to as the *First International,*

an organization made up of left-wing socialists, communists, anarchists, and trade unions. The focus of this alliance was on the working class and class struggle.

Refrain for *"L'Internationale"*
C'est la lutte finale
(This is the final struggle)
Groupons-nous, et demain
(Let us group together, and tomorrow)
L'Internationale
(The International)
Sera le genre humain.
(Will be the human race.)

The large number of students who turned out to support *Dany La Rouge*, as Cohn-Bendit was called because of his red hair and left-wing politics, and the others expelled from Nanterre was met by police who wasted no time attacking them with batons and tear gas. The students retreated, making their way back to the Latin Quarter where they tore up the cobblestone streets to use as weapons against the police. The stones were also used for building barricades to protect themselves from further attack. The violent rioting that occurred that day resulted in six hundred injuries among the demonstrators and 345 among policemen. From then on, May 6 was referred to as Bloody Monday.

Even though the government immediately banned all demonstrations, the riots continued over the next few days. Red and black flags hung on the sides of the Arc de Triomphe and *"L'Internationale"* was sung day and night. French citizens observing the appalling brutality employed by police sided with the students. Even the merchants whose businesses were impacted by the fighting on the streets around them were sympathetic. Women, workers, and ordinary people on the street helped students construct more than fifty barricades and gave them food, blankets, and other supplies. The unexpected camaraderie that developed between the demonstrators and their neighbors was extraordinary.

Although the students who had been arrested were released on May 13 and the Sorbonne was reopened, the major trade unions went on strike in support of the protests, demanding an end to the police brutality directed toward the students. They organized a march down the streets of Paris, with hundreds of thousands of marchers shouting "*de Gaulle Assassin*." Ironically, May 13 was the anniversary of de Gaulle's return to power after a twelve year absence following an attempted coup during the Algerian War of Independence that came close to bringing civil war to France. A number of students took advantage of the Sorbonne being reopened and decided to occupy it. Factories were also being occupied and the numbers of workers on strike increased daily at an astounding rate. Things went from bad to worse. The strike continued for weeks with half of the French labor force participating, somewhere between ten and twelve million workers. France was shut down. There was no mail delivery. Banks limited withdrawals in fear of having to close their doors. Public transportation came to a standstill. Garbage was not collected. Gas and food supplies disappeared. Eventually there was an effort on the part of strikers to deliver and maintain necessary services such as food supply, gas, and electrical power; but overall, things were a mess.

In the meantime, President de Gaulle worried that the government was in jeopardy of collapsing. On May 24, he addressed the country on national TV, calling for a referendum to confirm his ability to lead the country out of crisis as he had done in the past. Despite his plea, rioting continued. Some of the demonstrators from the Latin Quarter attempted to set the stock exchange building located on the other side of the Seine on fire. With everything that was going on, de Gaulle fled to Germany where one of France's military commands was stationed in the former French post World War II occupation zone of West Germany. Everyone speculated that his plan was to bring in the army to restore order to his country.

France's former general did return to his country a few days later, confident he had the backing of the military in case there was any attempt to invoke civil war. The mid-June referendum was called off and the National Assembly was dissolved. De Gaulle asked for a general election, vowing an end to the chaos that had threatened to bring down the government and proposing a generous wage increase. De Gaulle, gambling that voters would view his leadership more favorable than that of his socialist and communist opponents, captured sixty percent of the votes.

Things did calm down. The workers went back to work, leaving the students to figure out their next move. But without the support of the workers and the fact that summer vacation would mean fewer students demonstrating, there was no revolution in France. Disappointing for the students, perhaps, but the rest of France seemed satisfied to get on with their lives.

Those of us who were anxiously waiting to travel to Paris with Madame Girard breathed a sigh of relief.

Expressions of Revolt

During the May riots, art students as well as Marxist students and factory workers on strike occupied *l'École des Beaux Arts*, the premier art school in Paris. Together they established the *Atelier Populaire* (Popular Workshop) in the university's printmaking department where they produced thousands of posters with simple images and activist slogans depicting the growing discontent of the general public. None of the posters which were printed on colored newssheet via the school's silk-screening printing press bore the name of the artists who created them. When the workshop was set up, it was agreed by all that the artwork was a collective effort rather than an individual one. The raised arm with clenched fist stood for both solidarity and resistance while the depiction of a factory represented the role of workers in society. The posters were hung on barricades, carried by students and workers in demonstrations, and plastered all over France on buildings, light posts, and anywhere else they could be seen. Most of the posters had disappeared by the time I got to France, either pulled down by police or citizens who collected them as souvenirs.

LA BEAUTÉ

EST DANS LA RUE

Producing the posters was a highly organized twenty-four hour a day operation. Each morning striking workers and students met and collaborated on what theme to highlight that day. The design and slogans often grew out of their debate over current political movements and their collective desire to promote social change. The posters were mass produced then distributed by hundreds of volunteers. They were kept simple in design and bold in statement, a combination highly effective in delivering its message. As a result, what began with the protests of a few disgruntled students became a full-scale revolt with over ten million workers on strike and almost every factory and university in France being occupied.

Some of the more memorable posters included "The Beauty is in the Street" which shows a protester hurling a cobblestone at riot police in attempt to create a new society. The police were the enemy because their primary function was to uphold the laws and institutions aligned with capitalism and consumerism—everything the rioting workers and students sought to change. The French riot police are also credited for encouraging the violence

that ensued via their brutal attacks of students occupying universities and strikers in the workplace.

One of the best known posters of all was "A Youth Disturbed Too Often by The Future." It depicts a student of unknown race or gender wrapped in bandages. It is the victim's eyes that bring attention to authoritarian abuse being inflicted on those who oppose the status quo of the bourgeois culture.

Another poster, "Return to Normal" takes aim at those who wanted the struggle to end quickly so that everything could continue as it was—in other words, as it was meant to be in the minds of the conservative government and other conformists.

There were many other poster themes that grew out of the frustration shared by those who were involved in the revolt: poverty, unemployment, immigration, the Vietnam War, sexual freedom, opposition to the bureaucracy of President Charles de Gaulle as well as a society that had been entrenched in capitalism and consumerism since the end of World War II. Whatever the students and workers were against, there was a poster expressing their sentiments.

Only a person who never ventured outside could escape their message. They were everywhere and on everything.

The posters were not the only form of written protest. Walls, gates, sidewalks, stairwells, and buildings were stenciled with graffiti. Some of the slogans were proverbial; others expressed everything from discontent with French society, a call for radical change to the existing world order to outright anarchy. Many of the slogans were influenced by *Situationist International (SI)*, an international political and artistic movement dating back to 1957 that favored major social and political transformation.

Soyez realistes, demandez l'impossible
(Be realistic, demand the impossible)

One of the movement's most recognized slogans was written on a Paris laundry wall. It refers to the sand underneath the cobblestones that French students dug up to hurl at police in the May riots. City streets, regarded as a symbol of capitalism and consumerism by SI members, were transformed into canvases and words became the medium the protesters used to express their vision of social reform.

Sous les pavés, la plage
(Beneath the streets, a beach)

Two years before the riots in Paris, the SI movement put together a pamphlet known as "On the Poverty of Student Life." The pamphlet essentially called for student revolt against the establishment and its conservative values. It attracted leaders such as Danny Cohn-Bendit who circulated it among his fellow students in Paris. Some of the members of Situationist International took part in the occupations of the Sorbonne and also encouraged the occupation of factories.

The students who occupied the Sorbonne also took over the Centre Censier, the ultra-modern annex of the University of Paris, Faculty of Letters. The activists set up headquarters on the third floor of the building and formed an action committee for workers and students. Their objective was to seek out workers who shared a similar political outlook with the students. The two groups worked together to draft leaflets to target the specific concerns of factory workers throughout France. The leaflets were usually less than three hundred words in length. They would begin by listing any unsatisfactory working conditions such as wage, environment, safety or management, and end by inviting the workers to come to the Sorbonne or the Centre Censier to discuss their problems.

The leaflets encouraged workers to take control of everything within their industry in the same manner the students were attempting to take control of the universities:

France leaflet: *"Like the students, we must take the control of our affairs into our own hands."*
Renault leaflet: *"Our objectives are similar to those of the students."*
Rhone-Poulene leaflet: *". . . the students are challenging the whole purpose of bourgeois education. They want to take the fundamental decisions themselves. So should we."*
District leaflet (distributed in the streets at Boulogne Billancourt)**:** *"The government fears the extension of the movement. It fears the developing unity between workers and students."*

The action committee itself had no organized structure or fixed membership. Anyone could call a meeting, provided they had gathered enough interested people for that purpose. And once the meeting was called, anyone could propose what topic to discuss. There were no recognized leaders and points of action were developed in response to social situations, which were addressed in terms of what was possible rather than what was normal.

Every morning, the leaflets produced at the Censier campus were distributed by workers and students outside of factories and offices. They also passed out leaflets to citizens on the street. And every evening, the members of the action committee reported back to a general assembly what kind of reaction the distributed leaflet had received. Discussions would then follow to determine what modifications were needed for future leaflets. Nothing was kept from anyone. All information regarding discussions, decisions, and directives were published and distributed to both workers and students. It was this joint cooperation between two very different segments of society that helped disrupt the social order of France in 1968.

Flying to Paris

MY JOURNEY BEGAN early on the morning of July 1, 1968. I boarded a plane in Austin, Texas to Dallas and then from Big D to New York. I had only flown once and that was two years earlier when I visited a friend who had moved to Colorado. I loved flying back then, and I still remember the red sheath dress I wore on my first flight. My black patent belt matched my shoes and purse and I also wore a black hat and gloves. The flight attendants back then looked like they belonged on the runways of a Paris fashion house. It was different then. Flying was elegant. I was the only passenger in my row of seats on the flight to New York. That was another difference back then—large planes flew almost empty; not like today with every seat taken and sometimes double booked. I remember one of the flight attendants sitting down beside me and asking me where I was headed after spotting the passport I had left on the empty seat next to me.

JFK International Airport was overwhelming. Somehow I managed to get from the terminal where I landed to the one where my flight to Paris was scheduled for that evening. I was so relieved when I spotted Madame Girard at the gate waiting area. I did not know any of the other girls who were part of our group. Altogether, there were about fifteen of us traveling to Paris with Madame Girard. A few of them were not full time students at the university, a requirement for participating in the program at the Sorbonne. One of the girls indicated that the rules had been bent to attract more students in order to keep costs for the trip at a lower level.

The flight over was memorable only because of its unpleasantness. I lost a contact lens somewhere in the plane when I tried to remove them to avoid getting an abrasion. But I had worn them too long, so both of my eyes experienced intense pain and blurry vision that left me virtually unable to read anything. Despite my misery, I did enjoy getting acquainted with two of the girls in our group who were sitting in the same row of seats as me.

Penelope was the more interesting of the two. She had beautiful dark, almost black, long hair and her cheeks were naturally rosy. She was sophisticated, perhaps a year or two older than me. We seemed to like the same things: poetry, music, and art. The main difference between us was that she knew more about the things we had in common than me. But I was okay with that.

"Didn't we just have dinner an hour ago?" Sarah, my other seatmate, asked when the flight attendant asked us what we would like for breakfast.

"I think they are trying to keep up with the time change as we fly from zone to zone," Penelope observed.

"I can't eat anything else." I placed my hands on my overstuffed stomach.

"Wait till you get to Paris; everything is so delicious you will want to eat all day and night," Penelope responded.

"Oh, you've been to Paris before?" I inquired.

"No, but my aunt has, and she told me about the wonderful things she ate and how pleasant it was to dine in a country where food is more of an art than a necessity."

"Sounds rather fattening," Sarah noted.

"Not at all," Penelope replied. "The French eat very well, and you hardly ever see anyone who's overweight. It's what and how they eat that make a difference. Plus they walk and ride bicycles a lot."

I was beginning to feel a little nauseated from everything I had eaten since our flight began. I wasn't sure if it was from the food or motion sickness kicking in. I tried to sleep, but my eyes hurt so much I couldn't. Passengers chatting with one another as they lined up to wait their turn to use the restrooms also kept me awake. It had been a long day, and I was eager for the trip to be over.

As we were making our initial landing approach at Orly Airport, the plane shook violently, almost jolting me out of my seat.

"What was that?" I asked as the plane began a rapid climb back into the clouds.

"I think the landing gear jammed," Sarah said as she leaned over to get a better look out the window. We were sitting near the wing, so there wasn't much to see.

My eyes were in too much pain, and I was too tired to be scared. *Damn*, I thought. *We can't crash. I haven't seen Paris yet.*

We circled a few times before hearing the landing gear lock in place. Everyone let out a collective sigh of relief as the pilot began a gentle descent from the clouds. Our flight finished with a safe and smooth landing. It hit me then that I was in Paris, the City of Light and the City of Love.

It took a while for everyone in our group to get their luggage and go through customs. We then took a bus into the city, going immediately to the location where registration for classes was taking place. We had to bring our luggage with us since we did not have time beforehand to drop it off at the dormitory where we would be staying. To our disappointment, the Sorbonne had been closed due to the riots. Instead, our classes would be taught in a school across the street, the Lycèe de Louis de Grand.

"Votre nom, Mademoiselle?" one of the school administrators inquired.

"Je suis Patricia Taylor."

"Ah, oui. Et quels cours préférez-vous?" The classes offered at the American Summer Course included French grammar, conversation, literature, and civilization.

"I guess I will take . . ."

"En français, Mademoiselle; en français!"

I knew the administrators could understand what I was saying, but they refused to let us speak English and scolded us if we tried. It made signing up for classes difficult. I wasn't particularly interested in any of the classes offered. Even though I didn't feel comfortable with it, Madame Girard convinced me to take the advanced grammar class. I also signed up for French Civilization since it was taught in English. I wasn't too concerned about that since I had convinced myself that just being in Paris for the summer was an education in itself.

I was exhausted from the long journey and my vision had not completely returned. All I wanted to do was sleep. The taxi we took to the dormitory was the last taxi I ever took in Paris. The driver was insane. Five of us were crowded in his little Renault with most of our luggage sitting on our laps. I had the misfortune of being in the middle of the front seat, right next to the driver.

"I think I may be ill," I said to Penelope who was squeezed in between me and the car door.

"Well, don't throw up on me!" she said.

The most hair-raising part of our ride was circling the Arc de Triomphe. Everyone in Paris honks their horns to warn others about near misses and there were plenty of those.

"*Vous n'aimez pas le trafic à Paris, Mademoiselle?*" The driver laughed. "*Ne vous inquiétez pas; je suis un conducteur prudent.*"

Whatever he was saying to me in French wasn't very comforting.

The international women's dormitory we were staying at was called *La Vigie,* and it was located at 3, Rue des Carmes. Each of us was assigned roommates. Mine was a twenty-six-year-old woman who was married and very attractive. Anita was poised and spoke French with ease. I felt comfortable around her and the fact that she was older and knew more than me was like having a big sister by my side.

Our dormitory room was on the sixth floor. There were no elevators and the toilets and showers were shared by the entire floor. Our room had a little balcony with an iron railing. From the balcony, we could smell fish being sold somewhere in one of the street markets. But the room was comfortable, having twin beds and little else. Each day I climbed the six flights of stairs about seven or eight times.

La Vigie was run by a group of Catholic nuns. Every morning began with slices of freshly baked French baguettes purchased from a nearby *boulangerie*. We spread each slice with *La Vauche Qui Rit* (The Laughing Cow) cheese and drank large bowls of *cafè au lait* (coffee with hot milk). It was a simple meal, but one I looked forward to each morning. Sometimes I ate as many as ten slices of bread and drank two bowls of coffee, the equivalent of three cups each.

Each of us was given our own linen napkin. After each meal, we bound our napkins with a ring and stored them in a wooden compartment labeled with our names.

At home, I was used to having a clean napkin with every meal. Life at *La Vigie* was more frugal than fancy, but charming nevertheless.

Settling In

AFTER CLASSES LET out each day, we headed for one of the nearby sidewalk cafès on Boulevard St. Michel, commonly referred to as *Boul'Mich*. I either ordered a ham and cheese sandwich on baguette or a *Croque Monsieur*, a sandwich consisting of boiled ham between slices of *pain de mie* (soft white bread). It was then topped with grated cheese and grilled in a pan. It was yummy. I never tired of it.

I would often buy bread from a *boulangerie* and Brie or Camembert from a small *fromagie* to eat in my room for lunch or snack. The bread was freshly made and only lasted a day, but it was so much better than anything I had ever eaten in the States. Most of the girls from our group kept bottles of wine in their dorm room even though back home they were underage for drinking alcohol. I had not yet acquired a taste for wine, preferring Coca-Cola instead. But whereas a bottle of Coke cost around fifty-five cents, which was expensive back then, I could buy a bottle of table wine for about nineteen cents. A long loaf of French bread cost ten cents and cheese was not that expensive either. Despite all the bread and cheese I was eating, I never gained any weight due to all the walking I did going back and forth to class and climbing the stairs at *La Vigie*.

Dinner was served each evening at eight pm. An announcement was made over a speaker about five minutes ahead of time: *le diner est servi*. Most of the time, the meals were very good, especially the vegetables which were always perfectly seasoned with fresh herbs and butter. Occasionally we were served horse meat for our main course. On those evenings, I was vegetarian. The French have been eating horse meat as far back as the Revolution when it was necessary to avoid starvation. Later on, the surgeon-in-chief of Napoleon's army advised the troops to do the same if they wanted to stay alive. Eating horse meat was legalized by the French government in 1866 to benefit working-class citizens living in Paris who couldn't afford to buy beef or pork. A hundred years later, Parisians were eating it out of choice rather than necessity. I also do not eat seafood or fresh water fish, so when presented with a *poisson* with its head still intact and an eyeball staring at me, I would recoil, almost bolting from the table. The only way I could avoid eating it was to feign illness or allergy to certain foods, but I don't think the nuns who ran *La Vigie* really believed me.

The nuns kept everything in tip-top shape at the dormitory. Occasionally, they expected us to help with a few chores.

"Mademoiselle, porter ceci en bas pour moi, s'il vous plaît," one of them asked one morning as I made my way downstairs.

"Je ne comprends pas." I had no idea what she wanted me to do.

"Comme ça," she said as she took my hand and curved my fingers around the handle of a bucket filled with cleaning supplies. She then pointed downstairs.

"Ah, oui," I replied.

I was more than willing to carry the bucket downstairs for her. But was I ever going to understand what anyone was saying without them having to resort to sign language of some sort? I was frustrated and questioned how I could have

done so well in French class back home and still not be able
to understand a simple word or sentence any better than this.
Madame Girard told me not to fret too much. According to
her, all I needed was patience and practice.

The weather in Paris was a welcomed relief from the hot
Texas summers I was used to. It rarely got over 75° F during
the day and the nights were much cooler. The temperature
was perfect for all the walking we did. My classes took place
between ten am and one pm, so I had time each afternoon to
see and do whatever I liked. While some things had become
routine, there was always something new to discover and
enjoy in Paris.

All of the girls staying at *La Vigie* were invited to an
international dance and party held each month for foreign
students. One of the guys who asked me to dance was from
Greece. His name was Georgios, and he wasted no time
asking me to go out with him sometime. Madame Girard
would not allow us to go on dates, but she did let us hang
out with a few guys whom she knew and trusted, mainly so
they could watch out for us. A couple of them were in Paris
studying to be priests. They were fun to be around and one
of them was very attractive. Too attractive, I thought, for
someone who would one day take a vow to remain celibate
the rest of his life.

Georgios was not the only guy at the dance who wanted
my attention. There were two guys from French speaking
West Africa who also began a conversation with me. They
seemed to notice how uncomfortable I felt talking to them.
One of them asked me if I had ever spoken to a black man
before. I was totally shocked, but he was right. I never had. I
had spoken to black women who cleaned, ironed, or cooked.

But that was it. Although things were changing in the States and segregation was a thing of the past, racial bias was still alive and well and would be for a long time to come. I had been taught to stay away from black men and to fear them. What was meant to be a friendly conversation had felt more like a confrontation. Although I felt ashamed for the way I had reacted to them, I was also relieved when Georgios came to my rescue and asked me to dance with him again.

In Paris, women were openly admired. Whenever we came out on our balcony at *La Vigie*, the young men who lived in the building across from us would gape at us if they happened to be sitting outside their apartment. One day Anita took their picture to let them know we were aware they were watching us. They immediately went inside. Another time, we hung our lingerie to dry on a line we had strung across the balcony just to give them something besides us to look at.

Initially, I never went anywhere alone in Paris. I was too unsure of my French, and I didn't know my way around. Anywhere I walked, especially if Anita was with me, men would follow close behind. Most of their attention was directed toward my roommate, not me. She was an attractive woman who had an air of confidence about her that men found hard to resist. I was a shy school girl who hadn't lived long enough to be interesting.

"Avez-vous besoin d'un compagnon, Mesdemoiselles?" the men would ask.

"Merci, mais non," Anita would reply

"Nous pouvons vous montrer les meilleurs sites de Paris." They would insist on showing us around the city.

"Laissez-nous seuls, je vous prie." Anita would politely reject their offer.

Every day I spent in Paris was a new and interesting experience. I was even getting used to unwanted attention. Most of all I loved the sights, sounds, smells, and tastes that kept coming at me from all directions. My life in Texas seemed dull in comparison.

La Vigie was in the Latin Quarter, where all the hippies hung out. On my daily walks to and from class, I would see old men sleeping on the sidewalks. Some of them carried soiled mattresses with them. Between 1945 and 1968, about half of France's rural population had migrated to its cities and towns. The increase in city population, fewer jobs and/or lack of job skills had all contributed to the homelessness that we encountered on the streets. Based on their appearance, I think some of the hippies may have slept on the streets, too.

One day we walked past a group of bearded men wearing worn-out jeans and T-shirts. One of them handed us a pamphlet full of socialist/communist propaganda.

"What are they doing?" I asked. A couple of the men had managed to climb up on top of the roof of a building.

"They're raising the Soviet flag," Anita explained. "I guess they want to make a statement."

"What more do they need to say?" I asked. "The sidewalks are covered with graffiti."

"It'll be gone before long, just like the posters that were everywhere in May," Anita added.

Another day we passed President De Gaulle's mansion. There was a high wall surrounding the house which prevented the public from seeing that much. As I tried jumping up and down outside its gate to get a glimpse of what was inside, I felt a tap on my shoulder. I turned to see a *gendarme* with a big grin on his face.

"*Mademoiselle, avez-vous besoin d'un coup de main?*" he asked, mocking me by cupping his hands like a stirrup.

"*Ce n'est pas necessaire,*" I said and quickly moved away, embarrassed that I had been caught trying to get a peek of the president's mansion.

"I'm sure there are others who have done the same thing as you," Anita said. "The *gendarme* and his buddies are probably having a good laugh. They probably need one after all they've had to deal with lately."

There had not been any trouble that I was aware of since our arrival in France. There were places we went where whole sections were surrounded with *gendarmes*. They would show up in buses if they suspected any trouble from the communist students who mostly hung out in the Latin Quarter. The city had already begun paving the cobblestone streets near the Sorbonne that protesters dug up in the May riots.

We were beginning to hear rumors, though, that more riots would likely take place on July 14, Bastille Day. Madame Girard had secured invitations for us to attend the annual parade down the Champs-Élysées. It was supposed to be headed by President Charles De Gaulle, but with so many threats being made against him, it was uncertain if he would show up. I had promised my father I would take a photo of de Gaulle if he did take part in the parade. We were advised not to go, but several of us planned to anyway.

A few days before the national holiday, Madame Girard presented us with pink colored invitations for attending the parade. We had to insert our name on the blank line of the invitation. The card also instructed us to arrive by foot forty-five minutes early at the specified location.

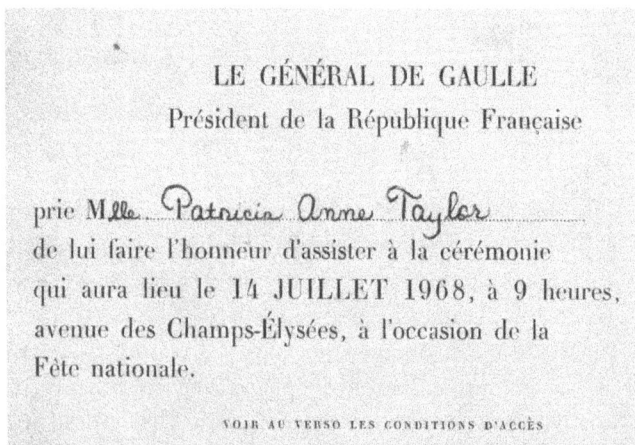

LE GÉNÉRAL DE GAULLE

Président de la République Française

prie Mlle *Patricia Anne Taylor*
de lui faire l'honneur d'assister à la cérémonie
qui aura lieu le 14 JUILLET 1968, à 9 heures,
avenue des Champs-Élysées, à l'occasion de la
Fête nationale.

VOIR AU VERSO LES CONDITIONS D'ACCÈS

As excited as I was about going to the parade, I couldn't help but think back to another parade that ended in tragedy in 1963.

"I don't like all the threats we keep hearing. It reminds me too much of what happened in Dallas to President Kennedy," I said as Anita and I filled in our names. "I was at the parade back then."

"Were you?" Anita asked. "Did you see what happened?"

"No, we left after the president's limousine drove past us. I'll never forget how radiant he looked and how beautiful Mrs. Kennedy was. Mother let me skip school that day so I could go to the parade. Two of my friends came with us. We were home before we heard the news. It was so terrible."

"I remember exactly where I was when I heard about it. You never forget things like that," Anita said.

In many ways, what happened in 1963 contributed to what was happening in 1968 worldwide. Not only was 1963 the year JFK was assassinated and Martin Luther King, Jr. delivered his famous "I Have a Dream" speech, but also the year Beatlemania was born after the Beatles released their first album. The pop culture phenomena this rock group helped create influenced young rebels around the globe to go against the established order. Everyone wanted change. They wanted new ideas and more benevolent leaders. In countries under oppressive rule, protests were directed at the state; while in America, the target of discontent was capitalism and the Vietnam War. In France, overcrowding in universities coupled with student demands for sexual freedom is what fueled the violent demonstrations that nearly ended in revolution.

News to and from Home

A FEW DAYS after arriving in Paris, I received my first letter from Ted. I couldn't wait to open it, but when I did, my heart sank.

> *I am not going to school this summer, I am going to Hawaii with Susan. Her mother is paying for the trip and has made it clear I have no obligation to her daughter. The only reason Mrs. Gray asked me to accompany Susan was because she had had a back operation and wasn't able to make the trip herself. Please believe me when I say I love you and I'm only going on the trip as Susan's escort. She's a friend, and nothing else. You are the one I love.*

Susan and Ted had dated off and on in high school. I was sure her mother would like to see them get back together and what better way than this. Mrs. Gray was a wealthy woman; it was nothing to her to pay Ted's travel expenses to and from Hawaii. I felt like the wind had been knocked out of me, but there wasn't anything I could do about it other than fret. Thank God I was in Paris. I hope that would be enough to keep my mind off of Ted and Susan spending time together on a tropical beach in paradise. I had thought Ted would be on a farm all summer, away from all temptation. This was what I got for being so smug.

From the time I told him I was going to France, Ted worried about my safety. But it wasn't the possibility of more riots that worried him, but the possibility of my being kidnapped and sold into prostitution.

> *I do worry about you—the white slave market of Europe is no joke and is anything but funny. Hundreds of girls disappear every year. Yes, many of them are kidnapped. They aren't used for slaves as you may think. They are used in prostitution palaces. You think they could easily get word out for help. Their rooms are usually bugged by microphones and they can tell if a man is trying to help one of the girls escape. The movie "House of a Thousand Dolls" was based on a true story about a girl that disappeared. It isn't a fantasy. It really happens. Please be careful and stay in a group.*

Ted constantly wanted to assure me about his upcoming trip to Hawaii. Being in France made it easier for me to deal with his being on a trip with Susan. Had I been sitting at home, I would have imagined the worst things possible.

> *I hope you won't be upset with me about Hawaii. It was kinda like France was with you; everyone was so excited about my going that I agreed before I really thought about it.*

Despite being in one of the most beautiful and exciting cities in the world, I missed Ted. I had received another letter from him updating me about his trip. He was scheduled to leave on Wednesday and would also get to stop over in

Disneyland and Hollywood. I was really glad he was getting to go on the trip, even if it was with Susan. Perhaps he would stop worrying about me being in Paris.

It wasn't long before I was receiving three or four letters a week from Ted. I was also writing to him almost every day, usually at night after dinner since we rarely went out after dark. If we did, it had to be with Madame Girard's approval. A couple of times, a few of us did sneak out for a few hours. The nuns usually knew when we came and went, but they never said anything to Madame Girard. They were cool when it came to minding their own business.

If I did have any doubts about how Ted felt about me, his letters should have convinced me otherwise.

> *I just want to talk to you so much. I love you. I've never missed anyone like I miss you. Sometimes (like now) I just don't think I can last two more months.*

I wrote long letters to my parents, too. I described in detail every place I went and all the things we did. My letters were written on thin blue airline paper to save on postage. We didn't have computers or cell phones back then, so everything was written in longhand. I wasn't able to call home since we also didn't have phones in our dorm rooms and it was expensive to make an overseas call. My parents could call me on the house phone at *La Vigie*, but the time difference and my varied schedule made it difficult to get in touch with me. It usually took several days for air mailed letters to be delivered. By then, most of the news either one of us received was outdated. Some of the letters I wrote to my parents did little to keep them from worrying about me:

You don't have to worry about riots while I am here because the French students aren't going to do anything until September when all of the students (about 500,000 of them) are back in Paris. They are planning a civil war, so this summer they are busy making bandages and setting up hospitals. They really don't have time to riot.

My mother's letters gave me something to worry about, too. My father was ill and needed surgery. Mother hadn't said what was wrong with him, but the bit about surgery didn't sound good. My being so far away from home made everything seem more imminent and dreadful.

In every letter she wrote, I sensed Mother was not telling me the whole story about my father. Not knowing something is often worse than knowing the truth. My parents had tried to keep the fact that my brother was dying back in 1964. I still felt betrayed by that. Now, with whatever was going on with my father, I felt left out in the cold, just as I had when my brother was ill. I wrote home frequently expressing my concern:

Daddy, I hope you're doing better by the time you get this letter. I've been worried about you—I hate being so far away from home with you in the hospital. Paris is really great; much better than I expected. I can never thank you enough for letting me come.

Later I learned that what I wasn't being told was that my father had only six weeks to live unless he had surgery.

I also wasn't told that once he was in the hospital operating room he decided not to undergo surgery at all, even though his doctors were convinced he needed it to save his life. He suddenly sat up and refused anesthesia. Soon after, whatever was wrong with him miraculously disappeared.

> *Dear Mom & Dad,*
> *I got your letter this afternoon. Glad to hear Daddy is home and feels better . . . There is only a week and a half of school left. I take my final on Saturday, August 3, and then am completely through.*

It was a relief to know my father was well enough to come home. I could enjoy the rest of my time in Paris now.

Getting Around

THE CITY OF Paris is divided into twenty neighborhoods, or *arrondissements*—a word that stems from the French verb *arrondir* (to encircle) due to the spiral layout of the districts. Each of these administrative districts is split into quarters that have their own names, as well as their own police station. Knowing this made getting around in Paris relatively easy.

Most of the street signs in Paris show the arrondissement in Roman numerals.

The last two digits of the city's postal codes also indicate the number of the arrondissement. I had begun to associate each district with the attractions it had to offer. *La Vigie*, where I was staying, was in the 5th Arrondissement in the section known as the Latin Quarter. This is where the Sorbonne and the Panthéon were also located.

Walking from *La Vigie* down the crowded *Rue des Carmes*, I could see the side view of the Panthéon's dome crowning what was originally a church built in the eighteenth century. This neoclassical jewel sits on a hill overlooking the left bank of the Seine River. King Louis XV had it built in honor of Sainte-Geneviève after surviving an illness that almost took his life.

Today, the building serves as a mausoleum where distinguished French citizens and national heroes are buried. Some of the most notable individuals interred there are

Voltaire, Jean-Jacques Rousseau, Victor Hugo, and Marie Curie.

I was also becoming familiar with navigating the city on the Métro, the rapid transit system of Paris. The trains ran mostly underground and were easily accessed.

Even the transit maps were easy to understand, with each line identified by number and color. We could go to most places in the city in thirty minutes or less. Penelope and I often used our time on the train to discuss our favorite poets and other literary figures.

Most of the time, we walked to where we wanted to go. There were so many sites within walking distance of *La Vigie* and traveling by foot was a good way to find unique shops and cafés. In addition, it made it easier for us to change our plans if we came across something that interested us more than our intended destination.

After class each day, Anita, Penelope, and I would stroll through *le Jardin des Tuileries* if the weather was nice.

"What are we doing today?" I asked my companions one sunny day as we sat in the chairs overlooking the beautiful gardens while eating our lunch.

"Well, Mademoiselle Renoir, how about *le Jeu de Paume*?" Anita teased.

"Don't call me that. I hear enough of it from Madame Girard," I complained.

"Sorry, I couldn't resist. Anyway, *le Jeu de Paume* has the best collection of Impressionist paintings in Paris. I love Renoir's "Young Girls at the Piano." I bet it's the one that inspired Madame Girard's nickname for you. We could also visit *le Musée de l'Orangerie* if you prefer."

"*Jeu de Paume* gets my vote," I said. Penelope nodded in agreement.

We finished our lunch and then wandered over to the museum. As we walked across the grounds, I noticed how different the people in the park were from the radical looking hippies we encountered daily in the Latin Quarter. There were young mothers who had brought their infants in baby carriages. Often they would sit and read, enjoying the fresh air and sunshine as they occasionally rolled the carriage back and forth to soothe a fussy child. Little boys wearing shorts and suspenders used long poles to push toy sailboats across one of the garden's ponds. Children leaned over the pond's edge to feed the ducks. No one was ever in a hurry. They walked slowly, taking in their idyllic surroundings with great pleasure. Being in such a peaceful setting took away any concerns I had about my father, my studies, or the possibility of more riots erupting.

From Russia with Love

MOST OF THE time, I was never alone when I ventured out in Paris. But one afternoon Anita and Penelope had other things to do, so I decided to stroll through the *Tuileries* without them. I stopped first to get a *Croque-Monsieur* for lunch, taking it with me so I could sit in the park and enjoy the abundant sunshine. It was a nice day. I finished half of the sandwich and placed the remaining half on the bench beside me.

For a while, I closed my eyes halfway and day dreamed, hardly aware of anything going on around me other than two birds fighting over crumbs near my feet. I pinched off a small corner of my sandwich and threw it on the ground. As I watched the birds scramble to get their share, two pairs of boots planted themselves in front of me. I looked up at two tall men with heavy beards smiling down at me.

"Bonjour, Mademoiselle. Are you enjoying your vacation?" one of them asked.

I was naïvely impressed that he knew I was a tourist.

"Very much," I replied.

"It's nice to meet you. My name is Yuri and my friend is Mika. What state are you from, Mademoiselle?"

I was even more impressed that he knew I was from the United States.

"Texas. And what state are you from?" Despite having foreign sounding names, I assumed Yuri and Mika were American since Yuri had no detectable accent and spoke perfect English.

"We're not from the States," Yuri responded.

"Oh, well, you must be from Canada."

"No, not Canada." Mika spoke with the same perfect English as his friend.

"I had no idea you were British." I felt as if they were playing a game with me.

"That's because we're not British," Yuri stated.

"Well, you really had me fooled. I would have never guessed you were French."

"You are wrong again, Mademoiselle," Mika corrected me.

"Then where are you from?"

"Russia," Yuri and Mika said at the same time.

"Russia? I didn't know they let you out."

I was immediately embarrassed for having made such a stupid comment. Neither Yuri nor Mika responded. I couldn't tell if they were amused by what I had said or incredulous of how naïve I was.

"What are you doing here?" I wanted to know.

"We are here to participate in the struggle between the citizens and the government," Yuri explained. "We would like you to attend one of our meetings. You should come with us."

"No. No, I can't do that," I replied.

"Why not? Don't you care about what is happening here, and in the world?" Mika prodded.

"Of course I do. But I have been warned not to get involved."

"Warned by whom?" Mika asked.

"My chaperone Madame Girard and the administrators at the Sorbonne warned us not to get involved with the protests. We will be sent home if we are arrested. We're not even supposed to take photos if there is another riot. We can be arrested for that, too."

"Join us. You will not be arrested. You are a student at the Sorbonne? Then you should want what is right for all students."

Initially, the French Communist Party (PCF) condemned the students at Nanterre University who broke into the Dean's office on March 22 to protest the recent arrest of several students during an anti-Vietnam War rally in Paris. These hooligans, according to the PCF, were not true revolutionaries. But as the March 22 movement expanded to include the workplace, and rapidly at that, the communists began to support it. Yuri and Mika were working for the

Party, attempting to recruit new members; especially from the ranks of young and credulous students like me.

As persuasive as comrades Yuri and Mika were, I refused to go to their meeting. I wasn't totally convinced that someone from Russia could speak English as well as they did. For all I knew, they could be members of the white slave market Ted had warned me about.

"Are you going to eat the rest of your sandwich?" Yuri asked.

"No. I've had enough."

"May I?" he asked, reaching for what was left of my *Croque-Monsieur.*

He quickly wolfed it down. Sharing my sandwich with him was about as close to communism I had ever come. I thought back to the "duck and cover" civil defense drills we practiced in school in case the Soviet Union launched a nuclear attack against us. We would crouch under our desks with our hands covering the backs of our necks, as if that would save us. It was all hysterical hype.

"So are you coming with us or not?" Yuri asked after consuming my sandwich.

"No, but thanks for inviting me," I said.

"Perhaps we will see you again, Mademoiselle. Enjoy your stay in Paris," Mika said.

I watched the two burly men walk away. I couldn't wait to tell Anita and Penelope what they had missed this afternoon.

Favorite Places

I HAD NEVER been in a place that had so much to offer in the way of culture. Paris was a visual feast, rich in history and intellectually stimulating. Nothing like what I was used to in Texas, where life was more casual and unpretentious. We didn't have medieval castles and universities that were centuries old in cities like Dallas, where the most iconic landmarks were the flagship building for the plush retailer Neiman-Marcus, The Adolphus Hotel, and the Magnolia Building with the Pegasus (flying red horse) perched on top.

I especially liked spending time at the Louvre which housed much of France's national treasures. From the time I was a young girl, I had dreamed of being an artist. The summer after my brother passed away, my mother enrolled me in Dallas Art Institute to keep me from dwelling on things I had no control over. I would spend the entire day, two or three times a week, with young professionals who were learning their craft. I was only fifteen, so I was not allowed to attend school on any day that nude models were scheduled to be there. Although I liked sketching horses and fashion models, my main interest was interior design. The director of the institute showed my work to a prominent interior designer in Dallas who later wrote me a letter offering me an apprenticeship once I graduated from school. Not realizing what a golden opportunity this was, I never followed up with him. But life is full of choices and had I accepted his offer, most likely I would have missed out on coming to Paris to study at the Sorbonne.

The Louvre dates back to the twelfth century when it was a fortress. Later, it became the home of French kings. In 1682, Louis XIV moved his household and court to the Palace of Versailles. The royal collection remained at the Louvre, which was occupied for a hundred years by the Royal Academy of Painting and Sculpture. Following the imprisonment of Louis XVI during the French Revolution, the former palace was designated as a public museum and the royal collection it housed became national property. A year later in 1793, the museum officially opened. Today, some of the world's most treasured art collections are held inside its walls.

Being around so much art was exhilarating. It is impossible to see all of it in one day. The painting I wanted most to see, the *Mona Lisa*, was also one of the most disappointing, mainly because of its size. I had always envisioned it as larger than life. There were so many other famous works of art that made up for it, though. One of my favorites was Jacques-Louis David's painting of Napoleon crowning himself as king; a whopping thirty-three feet wide by twenty feet high.

The best known landmark in France is the Eiffel Tower. I was amazed at how tall this wrought iron lattice structure was, about eighty-one stories high, making it the tallest structure in Paris. It is the very symbol of France itself and what every tourist in Paris wants to see. That was not the case, however, when it was constructed as an entrance to the Universal Exhibition of 1889. Parisians hated it, calling it a "truly tragic street lamp" or a "mast of iron gymnasium apparatus, incomplete, confused, and deformed." But that all changed over time and it eventually became the center point for celebrations like New Year's Eve and Bastille Day. The tower has three levels, but I only went as high as the first level where we had lunch at one of the restaurants.

We went on excursions almost every weekend. One of the more interesting places we visited was Mont St. Michelle, a medieval village that sits on a mountain-island in Normandy, France. We traveled twelve hours by bus to reach the island, but some of that time was due to several stops we made along the way. Our first stop was the Château de Fougères, one of the largest medieval strongholds in all of Europe. It was built in the eleventh century and boasts thirteen towers and three enclosures for added defense. The third and innermost enclosure functioned as the protection of the *keep*, a large tower made up of fortified houses that served as a refuge or safety net should the rest of the commune and castle fall into the hands of an enemy.

Our next stop was Saint-Malo, another walled city in northwestern France located along the English Channel. The ancient town dates back to the first century BC. What made this site memorable for me was that the Atlantic was the first ocean I had ever seen. It was night when we crossed it on our flight over to France. The Atlantic's shimmering turquoise waters were more beautiful than anything I could have imagined.

Before leaving Brittany that afternoon, I bought two dolls for my nieces. The dolls were dressed in the old Brittany style. Each doll wore a traditional cap, a dress overlaid by an apron, and a lace-trimmed embroidered shawl. The costumes became popular after the French Revolution, distinguishing the Bretons from the citizens of the centralized French Republic. I was sure my nieces would love them.

The French countryside we passed along the way was very picturesque and a welcomed change from the bustle of Paris and the aftermath of its recent woes.

> *There were little thatched-roof houses scattered about and we passed farmers working in the fields. It was so unlike anything I'd ever seen.*

The timeless, poetic, and pastoral scenes I saw that day made me long for a more simple life. I could see myself living in a little thatched-roof house nestled on a lush, green hill somewhere in the countryside; doing little more than tending a small flock of sheep.

I felt like I was embarking on a fairy-tale island when we arrived at Mont St. Michelle. The commune is named after the island's monastery which dates back to the eighth century. The monastery and eleventh century abbey with its jutting spirals sit high above the shops and houses that are layered on the sides of the mountain below. There are narrow little cobblestone roads winding in and out of the village. Fishermen and farmers live in small houses just outside the commune's wall. Altogether, there were only 106 inhabitants on the island. That night we stayed at a small and charming hotel where dinner was served on a large outdoor table.

Anita and I got up early the next morning so we could walk around the island before having breakfast. The tide was out, making the island look like it was stuck out in the sand all by itself.

"Look at all the sea gulls," I said. "It's so beautiful here with the sun peeping through those pink clouds."

"Lovely," Anita agreed. "I wish we could walk out on the sands, but we'd better not."

We reluctantly started back up the hill to the hotel. The tides could be high at times, varying as much as forty-six feet between the high and low marks. Warning signs were posted all about, cautioning visitors not to venture out on the sands. In earlier times, the only way pilgrims could reach the abbey was at low tide. Drowning was a real possibility both then and now for anyone caught in the unpredictable incoming tides.

Back in Paris, I was constantly exposed to many new experiences. There was something to see and do nonstop. We saw Verdi's *La Traviata* at the Paris Opera and Molière's *Le Bourgeois-Gentilhomme* at Comédie-Française. The opera was in Italian and the play was in French, so I could not understand that much of either one. I had never been in a theatre as opulent as the Paris Opera. I felt magnificent just being in such a grand hall.

Notre Dame was beautiful with its rose windows, flying buttresses, towers, and pinnacles. I could remember being impressed with the small Catholic cathedral I sometimes attended in Texas with one of my friends. Its architectural features were austere compared to Notre Dame's gargoyles and portals flanked by elaborate Biblical sculptures. Anita snapped a photo of Sarah and me in front of Notre Dame. We were eating cones filled with Italian gelato, a favorite treat of ours. I sent the photo to Ted. His reaction was exactly what I had hoped for:

The picture made me so lonesome for you I just wanted to scream. I miss you so much . . . It seems like such a long time until September. I worry about something happening to you.

Another weekend excursion I especially enjoyed was a tour of the Loire Valley which is located in central France. The valley is lush with vineyards, orchards, and fields teeming with artichoke and asparagus which line the banks of the Loire River. The majority of wine produced in this region is white, but it does produce red, rosé, and sparkling wines, too. The principal grapes grown in the valley were Chenin Blanc, Sauvignon Blanc, Melon de Bourgogne, Cabernet Franc, Gamay, and Pinot Noir.

The Loire Valley is also known for its rich heritage of *châteaux* which number over three hundred. Most of them are from the Renaissance. We attended a sound and light show after dark with performances by actors, singers, and dancers designed to take us back in time when royalty lived in the grand castles in the valley. *Château d'Usse* was my favorite for having inspired Charles Perrault to write his classic romantic tale of "Sleeping Beauty" in the seventeenth century. It was a delightful summer evening. We sat on the lawn all starry-eyed as if a spell had been cast on us as we watched and listened. I have never forgotten how enchanted I felt.

There were many other places we visited, some more memorable than others. I was in awe at how young my country was when I compared it to France and other European countries. The United States was less than two hundred years old. Here I was surrounded by castles that were several centuries old, some of which were still being lived in by the families who owned them.

A postcard I received from Ted was a sweet reminder of how much we missed each other while I was in France and he was in Hawaii:

> *I miss you so much. Maybe life will have it so that these trips can be repeated but next time with each other. I love you.*

I hoped so, too. I would love to show Ted all of France one day.

Bastille Day

The whole time I was in Paris, Ted worried nonstop about the possibility of violence erupting again as well as my being kidnapped by white slave marketers in Europe. Many of the letters he wrote me expressed his concern.

Pat, be careful. I'm so afraid. If anything should happen to you this summer I don't know what would become of me. I'm afraid God will take you away from me just for meanness.

Ted also spoke of his concern for his own safety. I was certain some of his fear stemmed from having lost his brother less than a year ago. I could understand how he felt since I had experienced the same sort of loss. Life is unpredictable and very fleeting. Losing someone close to us makes us more aware of that.

Pat, I love you. Please believe that. I don't want to worry you but if something should happen to me, I'll always be near you and watch over you. I know we don't like to mention such things; but just in case I want you to know that. You will not be without me. I love you so much.

Things had been quiet in Paris since my arrival. The cobblestone streets around the Sorbonne were being paved with asphalt. As far back as the twelfth century, the stones had been hurled at royals and other authorities in times of conflict. To prevent this from happening again, de Gaulle had ordered all the streets in the Latin Quarter to be repaved.

> *They've been paving the road by the Sorbonne—it was cobblestone like all the other streets but by paving it the students can't dig up the stones anymore. I think they expect to have a lot of trouble this fall. The Sorbonne is completely closed, of course—we have classes at a school across the street—the Lycée de Louis de Grand.*

I wasn't sure how much information my parents received on the nightly news in the US about the situation here in France. Most of what I knew came by word of mouth since I seldom watched TV or read the newspapers in Paris. It was a challenge to keep my parents informed about what was going on without alarming them altogether.

> *Oh—this Sunday, July 14th, will be Bastille Day. There will be a parade down the Champs-Élysées with President de Gaulle. We have special invitations. A threat has been made on de Gaulle's life and we have been advised not to go—but will anyway. We don't know if they will have riots here or not. It is kept quiet. But if there are going to be any riots—it will be Sunday. Sometimes we go places where whole sections are surrounded with police—many busloads of them. All we know is they are expecting trouble. There are many communist students here—the other day they even raised the Soviet flag on some building. They*

pass out pamphlets all the time and write stuff on the sidewalks.

On May 13, as a show of solidarity between workers and students, a one day strike was called by France's largest and most powerful federation of labor unions, the General Confederation of Labor (CGT). The CGT, which was politically dominated by the French Communist Party (PCF), did not join ranks, however, with all the other trade unions which supported the continuation of the strikes and factory occupations that followed. The PCF called for calm and moderation, preferring to keep the focus on higher wages and other workplace concerns. With more and more factories being occupied, the communists put up notices denouncing the revolutionary student movement and calling the students divisive "stooges of the bourgeoisie." Both the communists and students wanted to oust President Charles de Gaulle and his party from government, but the PCF believed the best way to achieve this was by electing one of their own rather than through violent clashes like those which took place in May between the students and police.

De Gaulle offered the workers a large wage increase on May 24. Three days later, the CGT managed to negotiate an even bigger increase if the workers would end the occupations and strikes. The workers refused to resume working, leaving France's fate in their control.

Fearing that his government was nearing collapse, de Gaulle called for a general election on June 23. He demanded that the workers return to their jobs or he would impose a state of emergency which would give him the authority to send in troops to end the strikes by force if necessary. To everyone's surprise, de Gaulle won the election by a wide majority. The strikes ended and the workers went back to work. The students ceased their street demonstrations and the police took control of the Sorbonne. The spirit of revolution wore off. Without the support of the workers, the students felt isolated. For a few, however, the revolution that never happened was still very much alive.

I was disappointed when I woke on Bastille Day. It was raining. Not a good day for a parade, but a little rain wasn't going to keep me from going. We arrived at the spot designated on our Bastille Day invitation about an hour before the parade was to begin. Despite the gloomy weather, thousands of people were already lining the streets. Many families had brought their children to see the parade.

Bastille Day is a national holiday that commemorates the storming of the Bastille on July 14, 1789. The Bastille dates back to the fourteenth century when it served as a fortress for defending the city from the English during the Hundred Years' War. Later on it became a state prison. During the reign of King Louis XVI, it was regarded as a symbol of royal tyranny. It was there that anyone opposing the king was kept under lock and key. The storming of the prison by angry Parisian crowds in 1789 marked the beginning of the French Revolution.

Ordinarily, President de Gaulle would open the parade by reviewing the troops before heading for the Place de la Concorde where he and other members of his government would salute the French military parade as it passed them by. Because of numerous death threats against him, de Gaulle skipped the traditional review and watched the parade from a safer location. This was disappointing since I had promised my father I would take a photograph of the French president that day.

Since 1880, a military parade has been observed each year in Paris on the morning of July 14. French servicemen, cadets from military schools, army tanks, and military bands pass down the fashionable tree-lined Champs-Élysées. The parade begins at the Arc de Triomphe, a monument honoring the victories of Napoleon Bonaparte, and ends at the Place de la Concorde, the largest public square in Paris. It was here that King Louis XVI was guillotined and later, Marie Antoinette. The air is filled with the patriotic hymn of the French Revolution, "*La Marseillais.*" The hymn was later adopted as the national anthem of France. The parade offers an impressive display of military might and national pride.

The long contrails of nine military jets flying in formation streaked the skies above the parade. I was glad I had not listened to the warnings about attending the parade. It was a festive occasion that went without incident. I was looking forward to the fireworks that evening. I had no intention of staying away from that either. I was in Paris and what could be more Parisian than to celebrate its national holiday?

Fireworks and Tear Gas

After the parade, we walked back to *La Vigie*. The rain had begun to subside and was expected to end by mid-afternoon, in plenty of time for tonight's celebration.

Madame Girard frowned when we told her we were going out that evening.

"I don't think that's a good idea," she said.

"But Madame, we are in Paris," Penelope argued. "Bastille Day is the biggest celebration of the year."

"I know, but this year is different."

"Nothing happened at the parade," Penelope said. "And we were warned not to go there, too. There haven't been any problems since we got here."

"If you insist," Madame Girard gave in. "But only if Jacob and Phillip go with you; and also Mike and Steve."

We were only allowed to go out in the evening if we had an escort. Madame Girard trusted Jacob and Phillip since they were studying for the priesthood and she had known Mike and Steve's families for many years.

"Merci, Madame," Penelope said.

"Don't take any cameras with you," Madame Girard insisted. "You are not allowed to take pictures if there are any problems; understood?"

"*Oui, Madame*," we responded in unison.

Jacob and Phillip showed up after dinner to escort us to the fireworks display. We were to meet Steve and Mike at a fountain on Boul'Mich. We walked a short distance down Rue des Carmes then turned left on Boulevard Saint-Germaine. A large crowd was already making its way toward the Seine River to stake out a spot on one of the bridges. We hadn't gone far before we heard the sound of marching feet and the low rumble of male voices rising and filling the air. We turned to see a group of young men marching ten abreast approaching us from behind. They shouted *de plus en plus nous sommes furieux* with bravado, raising a clinched fist for added measure.

We moved off the street and onto the sidewalk so they could march past us. They had switched from chanting to singing "L'Internationale," the Communist Party protest hymn sung by students and workers during the May riots. I found myself caught up in its provocative pulse as I strained to understand the lyrics. Even without knowing what each of the words meant, their delivery was rousing enough to make me want to join the march and link arms with the protesters, even though I didn't share their leftist ideology.

The demonstrators, mostly socialist students, leftists, and communists, held the red communist flag upright by its corners on either side as they paraded down the boulevard. They wore either red or black arm-bands; red by the leftists and communists, black by the anarchists. Busloads of police showed up and position themselves on either side of the street, creating a barrier between the onlookers and protesters. The riot police were wearing black helmets and carried batons and shields. The whole scene made me nervous. Things could get out of hand, and quickly. The police allowed the protesters to continue their march. Everything remained peaceful and calm, so we continued our walk down Saint-Germaine until we reached Boul'Mich. We turned right and headed for the

Fontaine St. Michel, famous for its sculpture of the archangel Michael wrestling with the devil. Mike and Steve were standing by one of the two winged dragons located on either side of the fountain.

We decided the bridges near the Eiffel Tower, which offered the best view of the fireworks, were too far away and would be too crowded, so we settled on Pont Neuf, the oldest bridge on the river. We continued until we got to the quay that ran alongside the Seine. By then, the streets were very crowded, and we had to contend with other bystanders for the tight space on the bridge. I stayed as close to Phillip as I could.

Steve and Mike had brought along two bottles of wine and some paper cups which they filled so we could toast one another.

"New York?" a Frenchman standing across from us asked as we lifted our cups.

We all laughed at his presumption that any American who visited Paris was from New York.

"Hey, everyone," Steve said as he held up the empty wine bottle, "let's put a note in this bottle and launch it down the Seine."

"We'll need pen and paper," I said.

"No problem," Anita said as she pulled both from her purse.

We wrote the date and occasion on the paper and then each of us signed our names. Steve placed the note inside the bottle and dropped the vessel into the river below. We watched the bottle slowly drift away and then disappear into the water.

Steve opened the second bottle of wine and offered some to the Frenchman who had been watching us. We were having such a good time we failed to notice that the marchers we had seen earlier had stopped on the quay and were handing out pamphlets and addressing the crowds.

Suddenly, a loud roar erupted from the Left Bank. People were running and screaming in all directions. The protesters and pedestrians blended together in the thick throng of chaos. The riot police, in their long black coats and helmet goggles, followed close behind with their batons in the air, dealing blows equally to anyone they encountered.

A number of people trying to escape being beaten by police or trampled by the mob ran up on the bridge, forcing those of us who had already secured a spot on Pont Neuf into an even tighter space. I could feel the sweat and weight of bodies pressing up against me as I struggled to push my way out of the human prison that held me back. Once I managed to free myself, my fear of being trapped on the bridge set in. I panicked and ran toward the quay, even though that was where most of the fighting was still taking place. The Frenchman we had befriended earlier saw me break away and quickly came after me.

"*Ne courez pas, Mademoiselle,*" he said as he grabbed me by the arm. "*La police va penser que vous êtes avec eux.*" He pointed to the Left Bank which was now engulfed in pandemonium.

"I want out of here," I demanded.

"*Restez calme,*" he said as he led me back to my friends on the bridge.

Phillip immediately came over and took my hand.

"You're shaking," he said as he pulled me close to him.

"The police were hitting people with their batons for no reason at all," I said.

"Everything will be fine. I won't let anything happen to you."

I felt safe in Phillip's arms until I looked over his shoulder and saw a burly policeman headed our way. Several other riot police were not far behind. My stomach knotted as the first policeman raised his baton and struck Steve on the shoulder. Most likely, he thought Steve was one of the hippie protesters because of his beard. As Steve raised his hands to protect himself from another blow, Glenda Cole intervened.

"Leave him alone!" she shouted as she bashed the policeman with her purse. "He's an American. He is not one of them."

The policeman turned around, ready to pounce on whoever had walloped his back. When he saw Glenda standing behind him with her purse high in the air, he immediately lowered his baton and backed away. Steve dropped his hands and dragged Glenda over to where the rest of us stood. We were all trying to decide whether it was best to remain on the bridge or find a safer spot to wait things out. The riot police, unable to find anyone willing to oppose them, headed back towards the quay. We were relieved to see them go.

We ended up waiting on the bridge until almost eleven. The fireworks display we had come to see had either not yet begun or they were called off altogether because of the rioting that was taking place. Although things had quieted down where we were, we could hear ambulance and police sirens from several blocks away.

"What do you think?" Steve asked us.

"The rioting hasn't stopped," I said.

"And it could go on all night. I think we should head out. Mike and I know our way around enough to avoid any trouble spots."

"I agree," said Phillip. "Everyone, keep your eyes and ears open and stay close."

The smell of tear gas still hung in the air as we approached Boul'Mich. There was broken glass, spent tear-gas canisters, and debris from make-shift weapons used against the police everywhere we looked. We could hear screaming and shouting among protesters and police as they continued to clash in the streets not far from where we were.

"It's too dangerous," Mike decided. "We'll have to turn around."

We wound our way back across the Seine to the Île de la Cité and stopped in front of at the *Préfecture de Police* to kill some time. It seemed like the quietest and safest place in all of Paris since every available policeman was over in the Latin Quarter. By midnight, we were all complaining about how chilly it was and how tired we were.

We went back over the bridge to the Latin Quarter. Fighting had taken place on almost every street we traveled. Sidewalk cafés had been vandalized; their tables and chairs overturned and their windows shattered. The windows of vehicles had also been smashed, covering the streets with broken glass. Remnants of smoke rose from the streets where tear-gas bombs had previously exploded.

We spotted a café that was still open on one of the smaller, unfamiliar streets that had escaped the pandemonium. We all ordered hot *thé au rhum* (tea with rum) which Anita suggested for calming our nerves. By the time we left the café it was after one. We made it safely to *La Vigie* by zig-zagging our way around the Latin Quarter.

Throughout the night we could hear sirens, glass being broken, and tear gas bombs exploding. By morning, everything had quieted down. The insurgence was short-lived and little more than a reminder of what had taken place in May. That was the last of the riots in Paris 1968.

A Change of Plans

THE NEXT MORNING merchants were out in the streets accessing the damage to their businesses and cleaning up the mess left behind by the previous night's rumble in the streets. Neighbors and people on their way to work stopped to look and offer their help or encouragement. Having grown weary of the disruption the earlier demonstrations had brought to their lives, they shook their heads in disapproval. They no longer supported the student movement as they had done in May.

Everyone seemed to agree that the worst was over now that Bastille Day had come and gone. With the threat of more riots removed, I could enjoy my time in Paris. I was looking forward to the tour Madame Girard was arranging once classes were over. We would travel to the French Riviera, Switzerland, and then to Italy. Not everyone from our group was going; just me and two other girls. In order to keep the cost down, Madame Girard had also invited three American women who sometimes joined us on our weekend excursions to go on the tour with us.

However, by the end of July, all of my plans changed. I had decided to leave Paris as soon as school was out instead of going on the tour. Not only was I was homesick, but I was disappointed in the way the tour was shaping up.

*I'm unhappy about the tour because only one other
girl is going and the other four people who are going*

are old women. I have already been embarrassed for
Americans because of some of the things they have done
and I don't think I could stand to be with them on a bus
for two and a half weeks.

I dreaded having to tell Madame Girard about my decision. Once she refunded the check I had given her for the tour, I could go to the Air France office and purchase a new ticket to fly home the day after graduation. The new ticket would cost more than what I had originally paid for my round trip chartered flight, but I could make up the difference with the money intended for the tour. I wrote my parents asking them to change my domestic ticket for the final leg of my trip home.

As soon as I get confirmed reservations to New York,
I'll send my ticket (the one from New York to Austin)
and let you get it changed for me. That way I won't
have to worry about it when I get to New York, because
I have to go through customs and I doubt I would have
time. Anyway, don't do anything until I know for sure
what day I'm coming home.

After dinner that evening, I told Madame Girard about my change of plans.

"I've already made arrangements," she stated. "It's too late to drop out."

"Well, I'm sorry. But I don't want to go on the tour."

"And what will you do instead? Do you plan to stay in Paris until we fly home?"

"I plan to go back home before then."

"Well, that's disappointing news. You will be throwing away an opportunity you may never have again. I really can't see it."

"Maybe, but my mind is made up."

"I'm responsible for you while you're here. Do your parents know about this?"

"They're okay with my decision. I need to have the check I gave you for the tour back, though."

"Dropping out now impacts everyone else on the tour; the less people, the higher the cost. I really don't think I have an obligation to return your check."

"I'm sorry for the trouble I'm causing you and the others, but I need my check back."

"Don't expect me to help you with any of your plans for getting home. I will need written permission from your parents allowing you to leave before our scheduled return."

Madame Girard handed over my check. She had not cashed it so I was free to do as I wished with the funds sitting in my bank account in Austin.

The next day I went to Air France to exchange the ticket for my flight home. They would not refund my chartered ticket, nor would they accept my personal check to purchase a new one. I would have to request a refund for the chartered ticket directly from the travel agency in New York which had booked the flight. That was going to take too long. I needed a new ticket now. The agent at Air France suggested I go to American Express to see if they could help me.

I spent a good part of the day at American Express waiting to speak with someone. Each person I spoke to told me the same thing: they could not accept a check from a small regional bank in Austin, Texas. Each time I was turned down, I asked if I could speak to someone else. Eventually, I found myself in front of one of the company's high-ranking officers.

"Why are you here, Mademoiselle?" the man with a mustache asked as he leaned back in his chair.

"I'm trying to get home. I have been studying in Paris for almost six weeks. I have a return ticket home, but it does not leave until the end of August. That is too far off. Air France will not accept my personal check. I need a Travelers Cheque so I can buy a new ticket."

"May I see your check?"

I handed him my check. He studied it carefully then gave it back to me.

"I'm sorry, Mademoiselle. We cannot accept your check. If you were one of our customers we could possibly accommodate you. I trust you understand our position."

"The check is good," I insisted. "I have been here for hours and have talked to several people. All I want to do is go home." My lips had begun to quiver and tears were welling up in my eyes.

The man leaned forward and clasped his hands together on his desk while he waited for me to gain control.

"But you have a return ticket. Why is it so urgent for you to leave Paris sooner than your ticketed flight?"

"My father has been seriously ill. I don't know what is wrong with him. I just want to go home. I am so far away and all I do is worry."

The man sighed and looked away.

"We don't ordinarily do this, but I will make an exception. I believe you are sincere, Mademoiselle. It is a risk, but a small one."

"Thank you so much. I truly appreciate it."

Once I had the American Express Travelers Cheque in my hand, I went back to Air France and purchased a new ticket home. I would leave on August 10, one day after graduation.

Celebrations

I COULDN'T WAIT for classes to end. Finals would take place on August 3, the day before my birthday. We would graduate on August 9 and, according to Madame Girard, there would be a lavish ceremony presided over by officials from the American Embassy in Paris, the University of Paris, and the Ministries of Foreign Affairs and Education.

About half way through the study course, I had dropped out of French Grammar. As graduation approached, I realized how little effort I had made to improve my language skills. It was so much easier to let the French converse with me in English. I had also found the lectures in French Civilization boring. Madame Girard assured us that the final exam for the past several years had concentrated on the Hundred Years' War. Study that, she had advised, and we should do well. But even limiting my study to a series of conflicts between the rulers of England and the rulers of France over the succession of the French throne during the Middle Ages proved difficult for me. I didn't come to France to be bored; I justified my not putting more effort into preparing for the final exam.

Madame Girard ended up cancelling the after graduation tour once I dropped out. I could sense she blamed me for spoiling her plans, but I didn't let that bother me. Now that I knew I would be returning home after graduation, I was more relaxed. There hadn't been any more trouble in Paris since the riot on Bastille Day and that, too, added to my enjoyment of the city. We took boat rides down the Seine, visited museums, spent afternoons in the parks, had lunch at sidewalk cafés, and went shopping on Rue de Rivoli where I purchased Joy Parfum for my mother and a Christian Dior tie for Ted.

On August 4, my birthday, we set out early for Versailles. It was a beautiful day, and I was looking forward to spending it in the most elegant palace in all of France. The palace was originally built by Louis XIII as a hunting lodge. His successor, Louis XIV, enlarged it into a royal palace with lavishly landscaped gardens. Some of the cost for the expansion was paid for from the king's own purse; revenues which were essentially derived from his subjects in France as well as Canada. To appease everyone, the finance minister of France, Jean-Baptiste Colbert, insisted that all the materials and furnishings of the palace were made in France.

The Hall of Mirrors with its seventeen arches was one of the most opulent features of the palace. Each arch was augmented by twenty-one mirrors which reflected the windows overlooking the gardens. Finance Minister Colbert brought in artisans renowned for their craftsmanship from the Venetian Republic to France, where they constructed the hall's mirrors at the *Manufacture Royale de Glaces de Miroirs*. During the seventeenth century, the Venetian Republic held a monopoly on the manufacture of mirrors. In order to preserve technology secrets employed in the manufacturing of mirrors, the government ordered the assassination of the Venetian artisans once they returned to their homeland.

The Hall of Mirrors was the grandest thing I had ever seen. Everywhere I looked there were glass chandeliers, gilded statues, marble walls and flooring, and beautiful ornate scenes depicting Louis XIV's reign painted on the ceiling. There was no way I could fully describe how magnificent it was. Being there on my birthday made it even more special.

During the French Revolution, the royal family was forced to leave their palace home. After years of neglect, Versailles became home to the Museum of the History of France in the early part of the nineteenth century.

As beautiful and splendid as the palace was, I found myself drawn even more to the *Hameau de la Reine* (the Queen's Hamlet). The rustic little village was built for Marie Antoinette as a private meeting place for the queen. Its countryside setting with meadows, lakes, and streams is situated in the park of Versailles and included a farmhouse, dairy, mill, barn, and the queen's house. The cottage gardens were a jumble of natural charm and unruliness; a noticeable departure from the formal gardens of Versailles.

What interested me most was the reason behind the hamlet's existence. It was where Marie Antoinette would go to escape the responsibilities and duties of being queen. She would dress as a young shepherdess and pretend she was a peasant. The shepherdess queen would even milk the cows and sheep that were kept on the farm. Her closest friends were often invited to participate in her enjoyment of the simple life. Despite the pretense, the comforts of royalty were always close at hand.

The real peasants of France were offended by the queen's mockery and grew more and more resentful of her and the royal court. While they were starving, she was frivolous in playing like she was one of them. The peasants were equally incensed that their queen was spending a great deal of money to create and maintain her fantasy world at a time when the economy of France was so depressed. It was also rumored that the queen entertained lovers at her hamlet. The mounting resentment of the queen contributed greatly to the onset of the French Revolution.

As unpopular as she was, I found myself drawn to the queen and her fondness for an unpretentious lifestyle; perhaps because of my own desire to lead a more simplistic life. When we visited *La Conciergerie* in Paris, tears had rolled down my cheeks. It was as though I could feel the last Queen of France's presence still haunting the tiny cell where she spent her last days. I cannot explain it. *La Conciergerie* was where prisoners awaited the guillotine during the Reign of Terror, France's darkest period in history. Marie Antoinette was undoubtedly the jail's most infamous prisoner.

After leaving the hamlet, we strolled through the beautifully designed gardens of Versailles. There are about eight hundred acres of manicured lawns with shrub and floral plantings. The garden layout is all done in classic French style. There were multiple water features, pools, and sculptures which served as fountains throughout. During the reign of Louis XIV, one-third of the cost of building Versailles was due to the extensive water supply systems necessary for maintaining the lush gardens of the palace.

"Have you ever seen anything like it?" Penelope asked as she walked alongside Anita and me.

"Never," was all I could say. I only hoped the photos I took that day showed just how magnificent they were. We had nothing back home that even came close to this.

It was a good day for me. Surely, there was not a better place on earth than Versailles to spend my birthday. It would have been nice to have Ted with me today to celebrate. I wondered if he was thinking of me, too. Somehow, it felt like he was. Ted promised to get something for my birthday in Hawaii. I couldn't wait to see what it was.

We returned to Paris that evening. Following our evening meal at *La Vigie*, the nuns presented me with a vanilla cake to share with the members of our group. I was grateful that Anita and Penelope had found a tactful way to discourage the nuns from baking their traditional rum and raisin cake, which I truly detested. After Anita poured everyone a glass of Champagne, Madame Girard gave a quick toast. She then excused herself. She had been distant toward me since I bailed out of the tour and for once, she did not refer to me as Mademoiselle Renoir.

Anita, Penelope, and I thought about sneaking out for the evening like we had done so on several occasions after Madame Girard had retired for the evening. We usually stayed close by if our male escorts weren't with us. But tonight, we were too tired from our visit to Versailles. We stayed up a while longer until all the Champagne was drunk and we had eaten the last piece of cake.

Adieu Paris

I SPENT MY last few days in Paris visiting my favorite places: *le Musée du Louvre, le Jeu de Paume, le Jardin des Tuileries,* and strolling along the Seine. There were so many interesting and beautiful things to see that it was impossible to name them all. I felt a little sad about leaving, but at the same time I was anxious to get back home.

Anita and I carefully planned my "escape" from the clutches of Madame Girard. I had not revealed the date I was flying home because I knew she would try to persuade me to stay the full time, if for no other reason than to save face. My early departure would surely raise eyebrows about Madame Girard's ability to properly chaperone a group of young girls in a foreign country.

Anita and I rose early on the morning of August 10. I had packed my bags the night before so we could leave *La Vigie* around five in the morning, long before any of the others in our group were out of bed. We quietly made our way down the six flights of stairs and almost made it out the door before one of the nuns spotted us.

"*Est-ce que vous partez pour le weekend?*" she inquired.

"*Juste mon amie, ma sœur,*" Anita replied.

"*Avez un bon voyage.*" The nun smiled at me as she held the door open for us.

"*Merci, ma sœur,*" I said. I was glad that she had not asked where I was going.

Anita and I lugged my four suitcases to the Métro station a few blocks away for the ride out to Orly. Although Anita was staying in Paris a while longer, she had booked passage on a freighter for her trip home rather than going back on the chartered flight with Madame Girard's group at the end of August. I wasn't quite sure why she chose to do that. She never told me, but I suspected Anita and her husband were having difficulties. I had hoped to stay in touch with her once we were back in the States, but that never happened.

Anita helped me check in at Orly and then walked with me to the gate. I had about a three hour wait for my flight home. Anita wanted to get back to *La Vigie* before Madame Girard began to worry why neither of us had come down for breakfast.

"It's been a great summer, kid." Anita hugged me.

"It has; though I wish it had ended a little better," I said.

"Well, sometimes you have to do what your heart tells you to do."

"I know. Do you think Madame Girard will throw a fit when she hears I'm on my way home?" I asked.

"I'm sure she will. But don't worry about her. I'll miss you, Mademoiselle Renoir."

"You had to remind me." I laughed. "I hope I never hear that name again."

We said goodbye, and I watched her walk away. She turned one last time and blew me a kiss. Although I never saw her again, I never forgot her.

The flight home was better than the one that brought me to France. On one side of me was young woman who had been on spiritual retreat in France. She was preparing to take her initial vows as a Catholic nun. On the other side of me was a middle-aged Jewish businessman. I was Protestant, so we were about as diverse as you could get. But we had a good time talking with one another and discovering how much we had in common despite our different backgrounds.

A Frenchman who was sitting across the aisle about three rows up continuously turned in his seat and stared in our direction. It was a little unnerving.

"Why do you think he is staring at us?" I asked the young nun.

"He's looking at you," she said.

"Me? But why?"

"I think he finds you attractive."

I smiled. If Anita had been sitting next to me, he would have been admiring her, not me. It felt good to have all the attention for once.

It was late afternoon when we landed in New York. I still had to catch two flights before I would be home. I was happy, though, to be back in my own country.

I wasn't aware that Ted and I were returning from our trips on the same day. I received a letter from him a few days after I was home.

Well, I made it home safe. I've had a great time but it's nice to be home. I think we arrived home about the same time. We got to Beaumont just a little before 10 o'clock. A few of my postcards and a letter may never reach you. I don't see how you found the time to write as often as you did. Pat, even though I may not have written very much, I do love you. I have your birthday gift(s). I hope you like them.

I wouldn't see Ted until classes began in September. That seemed like such a long way off. But at least we were no longer thousands of miles apart. I could hardly wait to see him again.

September 15 seems to be a far-away time. We came through the summer and love one another more than before. The long time until when school starts doesn't worry me like the long summer did. I love you. I hope we will always need each other. I need you very much.

When I look back, it is difficult for me to think that I ever doubted how Ted felt about me. I had everything I had ever wanted the summer of 1968. I just didn't know it. I was privileged to visit one of the most beautiful cities in the world, to study at the Sorbonne, and to have the person I loved the most send me letters expressing how deeply he loved me. We don't always see what's right in front of us; or if we do see it, we don't realize how lucky we are. I know all of that now. And even though I never went back to Paris and eventually my relationship with Ted fell apart, the memories of both are still with me and always will be. Ted and I are still friends and Paris is waiting for my return. *Je reviens, Paris!*

Epilogue

I RETURNED TO Paris in October 2017; this time as a tourist with two of my friends. Although I was excited about going, I did not arrive in the City of Lights with the same wide-eyed innocence I had as a young girl about to embark on the experience of a lifetime. Paris, along with the rest of the world, has changed considerably since 1968. No one would argue that. It is still a beautiful city, though; an architectural feast of centuries-old styles that coexist alongside the stark contrast of modern day construction.

In 1968, there were no skyscrapers in central Paris other than the Eiffel Tower. With a height of 1,063 feet, this magnificent structure could be seen all over the city. No other building came close to rivaling its lofty reach of the sky. But then it happened. The Montparnasse Tower, 689 feet high, was completed in 1973. Since then, over seventy skyscrapers have bruised the skyline of central Paris and surrounding areas. Most of them are less than 500 feet tall. The tallest is Tour First. At 758 feet, it is surpassed in height only by the Eiffel Tower. There are a number of skyscrapers that have been proposed or are currently under construction; two of them almost as tall as the city's iconic wrought-iron lattice tower itself.

Between 1954 and 1999, the population of Paris declined steadily. This was largely due to residents moving to the suburbs. The most recent estimate of people living within the city limits is 2.3 million. The population of the surrounding suburbs is 10.5 million. Paris is a crowded city. As a result, there are more beggars and more pickpockets. There is more traffic, more new construction, and more noise. People walk around with their eyes glued to their cell phone screens rather than taking in all the glorious sights around them. I don't fault Paris for this. It's like that everywhere. But there is a sense of hurriedness now I did not see in 1968. Only in the finer restaurants and bistros do things slow down; including the service—but maybe that's by design. In Paris, cuisine is still an art and *bon appetite* is a promise.

There are other things, I'm happy to say, that haven't changed much since my first visit. Children still sail toy boats in the pools of the Tuileries. Wine is an essential part of dining and the French language has not lost its renown for being one of the most beautiful sounds in the world. The building where I stayed in 1968, the international dormitory *La Vigie,* has been converted into apartments/condos. I spotted the balcony of the room I shared with Anita on the sixth floor. I don't know if I will ever have the opportunity to visit Paris again, but my memories of being there will always remain in my heart. Everyone should go there at least once. *Adieu, Paris!*

References

Illustrations by Charles Hayes:

> page 15: Rally at Arc de Triomphe following de Gaulle's re-election
>
> page 21: Student riot in May following shut-down of Nanterre University
>
> page 23: Student/Worker Protest
>
> page 43: Gendarme outside of de Gaulle's mansion
>
> page 55: Russian activists
>
> page 72: Riot Police
>
> page 74: Riot on Bastille Day

1968 The Year that Rocked the World. Mark Kurlansky. New York, NY. Random House Trade Paperbacks, 2004.

1968: Workers Join Paris Student Protest. BBC On This Day: 13 May, 1968. http://news.bbc.co.uk

An Introduction to the Situationists. Jan D. Mathews, 2005. http://theanarchistlibrary.org

Arrondissements of Paris. https://en.wikipedia.org/wiki

Bastille Day. https://en.wikipedia.org/wiki

Beauty Is in the Street. https://en.wikipedia.org/wiki

Citroen Action Committee—I. F. Perlman. https://libcom.org/book/export/html/1854

Declaration of the Communist Representatives of the Paris Region. http://www.marxists.org/history/france/may-1968/paris-region.htm

Demand the Impossible. Mark Vallen, 2001. http://www.art-for-a-change.com/Paris/paris.html

Eiffel Tower. https://en.wikipedia.org/wiki

Egalité! Liberté! Sexualité!: Paris, May 1968. http://www.independent.co.uk

Everyone to the Barricades. Sean O'Hagan, 2008. The Guardian. http://www.theguardian.com/2008/jan20/1968theyearofrevolt.features

France: May-June 1968 and Today. Ulrich Rippert, 2006. World Socialist Web Site

Gardens of Versailles. https://en.wikipedia.org/wiki

Hall of Mirrors. https://en.wikipedia.org/wiki

Hammeau de la Reine. https://en.wikipedia.org/wiki

Horse Meat. https://en.wikipedia.org/wiki

La Conciergerie-Medieval Prison Where Marie Antoinette Awaited the Guillotine. http://www.coolstuffinparis.com/conciergerie.php

Les Beaux Arts Affichent dans la Rue: The Posters of L'atelier Populaire. Rhiannon Vogl, 2007.

Liberated Censier: A Revolutionary Base. http://www.lchr.org/a/41/m1/peract15.htm

Louvre. https://en.wikipedia.org/wiki

May 1968. http://counterculture.wikia.com/wiki/May_1968

May 1968 Events in France. https://en.wikipedia.org/wiki

Palace of Versailles. https://en.wikipedia.org/wiki

Panthéon. https://en.wikipedia.org/wiki

Paris '68: (1) An Anarchist History of the Events (2) An Eyewitness Account. http://flag.blackened.net/revolt/disband/solidarity/may68.html

Paris 68 Posters. http://libcom.org/gallery/paris-68-posters

Paris Métro. https://en.wikipedia.org/wiki

Paris Student Riots. (May 1968) http://histclo.com/fran/co-fran1968/html

Posters from 1968 Paris Riots. Bibliothèque Nationale de France. http://gallica.bnf.fr

Situationist International (1957-1972). http://jahsonic.com/SI.html

Sorbonne. https://en.wikipedia.org/wiki

The Art of the 1960s Paris Riots. http://www.messynessychic.com

The Internationale. https://en.wikipedia.org/wiki

Vietnam War. https://en.wikipedia.org/wiki

Patricia Taylor Wells published her first book in 2016: *Camp Tyler, A First of its Kind* for the benefit of Camp Tyler, the oldest outdoor education school in the country, which she attended as a child. Most of Ms. Wells' writing has been directed at serving organizations and causes important to her. As a result, she was selected to write the first article for the newly created Authors Among Us column in *Tyler Today Magazine* (June/July 2016). She also published two poems, a short story and a narrative non-fiction article in the 2016 East Texas Writers Guild Anthology.

She published her first novel, *The Eyes of the Doe*, in 2017. Prior to publication, the first chapter placed as a finalist in the 2016 First Chapter Competition for Historical Fiction sponsored by East Texas Writers Guild. Her article about the novel was featured in *Tyler Today Magazine* (October/November 2017).

Ms. Wells, who holds a BA in English and French, facilitated writing critique groups for the Atlanta Writers Club and Knoxville Writers Group. She especially enjoys writing poetry and draws inspiration from the wide range of experience she gathered from her travels and living in a variety of places. She currently lives in Tyler, Texas with her husband Bob and their dog Kaspar.

www.ingramcontent.com/pod-product-compliance
Lightning Source LLC
Chambersburg PA
CBHW031521040426

42445CB00009B/333

*9 7 8 1 9 4 5 8 0 5 0 1 1 *